The Reward for Work Well Done: Jonas Salk

Heidi Schoof

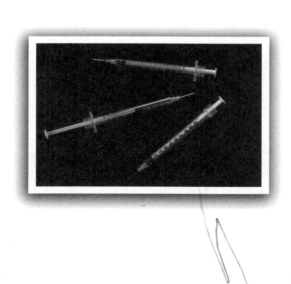

PACIFIC
LEARNING

© 2004 **Pacific Learning**
© 2004 Written by **Heidi Schoof**
Edited by **Rebecca McEwen**
Designed by **Anna-Maria Crum**
Photography: Library of Congress (cover, p. 4); National Library of Medicine (pp. 5, 8, 10, 13, 15, 17, 18, 26); Al Fenn/Time Life Pictures/Getty Images (pp. 7, 14, 23, 24, 27); Tore Johnson/Pix Inc./Time Life Pictures/Getty Images (p. 21); George Skadding/Time Life Pictures/Getty Images (p. 28); Tony Korody/Time Life Pictures/Getty Images (p. 29); Arnold Newman/Getty Images (p. 31).

08 07 06 05 04
10 9 8 7 6 5 4 3 2 1

Published by
    Pacific Learning
    P.O. Box 2723
    Huntington Beach, CA 92647-0723
    www.pacificlearning.com

ISBN: 1-59055-365-9
PL-7313

Printed in China.

Contents

Introduction: Polio

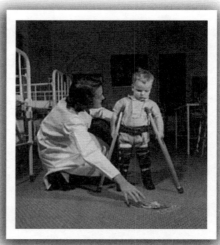

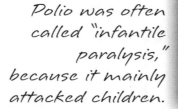

Polio was often called "infantile paralysis," because it mainly attacked children.

The first polio epidemic swept across the United States in the summer of 1916. In twenty-six states, more than 27,000 people were ill, and 6,000 people died. Sadly, most of the victims were children under five years old.

Doctors around the world struggled to treat polio. Unfortunately, no one knew what caused polio or how to prevent it.

By the 1930s, to most Americans, summer meant polio season. Cities all over the country closed swimming pools, movie theaters, and playgrounds. Parents kept their children away from crowds and public places. It was impossible to guess when or where polio would strike next.

QUARANTINE
POLIOMYELITIS

All persons are forbidden to enter or leave these premises without the permission of the HEALTH OFFICER under PENALTY OF THE LAW.

This notice is posted in compliance with the SANITARY CODE OF CONNECTICUT and must not be removed without permission of the HEALTH OFFICER.

_____ Health Officer.

Form D-1-Po.

Homes and entire neighborhoods were quarantined to try to control the disease.

A Good Beginning

Jonas Salk was born in New York City on October 28, 1914, less than two years before the first polio epidemic. He was a serious, well-behaved boy who got good grades in school. In fact, he was such a serious student, he raced ahead in school and entered City College of New York when he was only fifteen years old.

There, Jonas loved to study science, especially biology and chemistry. He liked the way scientists asked their own questions and then worked to find the answers. Jonas decided to become a doctor so that someday he could answer questions about what caused diseases.

After graduating from City College in 1934, Jonas enrolled in the School of Medicine at New York University.

Jonas Salk

While he was in medical school, Jonas studied **bacteria** and **viruses**. During the summer breaks, he worked in a laboratory.

Dr. Thomas Francis became Jonas's good friend.

He was especially interested in **immunization**. During his senior year, he worked with a new professor named Dr. Thomas Francis, who shared many of his ideas. Dr. Francis was working on a **vaccine** to control influenza. Jonas's job was to test the vaccine on lab mice.

Dr. Jonas Salk graduated from medical school in June 1939. He decided to work with Dr. Francis for another year, before he began his **residency** at Mt. Sinai Hospital in New York.

Jonas was an excellent doctor. He was well liked by his patients and coworkers. Still, lab work was his passion, and he chose to go into research when his internship ended.

Jonas went to work with Dr. Francis at the University of Michigan for five years. During this time, he learned all that he could about the **immune system** and how the body fights off diseases.

Dr. Jonas Salk

He knew that when a body fights off a disease, it usually becomes immune to catching that disease again. The vaccines that Jonas was testing were always made from the same kinds of germs that the body would try to fight. He learned the best ways to make a weak form of the disease – it had to be strong enough to trick the body into fighting it, but not so strong that it would make the body sick.

The more Jonas learned, the more he dreamed of having his own laboratory. He wanted to do what he thought best to help people fight off diseases.

The Poliovirus Program

Jonas Salk truly understood the horrible effects of polio. Hospitals had polio wards that were full of frightened children who couldn't move their arms or legs. Some, who couldn't breathe on their own anymore, lay in huge artificial breathing machines called iron lungs.

Although many children got well after having polio, thousands of children died. Others lived in beds or wheelchairs. Still others wore heavy leg braces and used crutches for the rest of their lives.

One of the main problems behind the spread of polio was that no one really knew what caused it. At first, people thought it was carried by houseflies, garbage, car fumes, or even ice cream and candy.

Polio actually spreads when people don't wash their hands well enough after using the bathroom, then touch food or other people. It can also spread through the water supply.

After having polio, some people had to stay in an iron lung for the rest of their lives.

Once poliovirus gets into the body, it attacks cells in the brain that send messages to the muscles. When the messages stop, the muscles can no longer move.

Jonas wanted to find some way to stop the progress of this dreadful disease. He took a job at the University of Pittsburgh in 1947.

He began working to find out what kinds of poliovirus really caused polio. The university gave him money to set up his own laboratory, buy the equipment he needed, and even to hire his own staff.

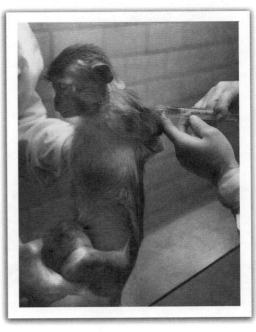

A rhesus monkey getting an injection

Dr. John Enders won the 1954 Nobel Prize in Medicine for his work.

At the time, scientists would give rhesus monkeys injections of different kinds of viruses. Results wouldn't be seen for months. Jonas was sure there had to be a better and faster way to get the job done.

Sure enough, in 1949, a scientist named Dr. John Enders found a way to grow viruses in test tubes in a lab. Before, the virus was always grown on a live animal.

Jonas was sure this new method would save time and money. He proved to the National Foundation for Infantile Paralysis (NFIP) that in only one week of using the new technique, he could do work that used to take months.

Developing the Vaccine

When Jonas had completed his work studying the three kinds of virus that cause polio, he began to devote himself to making a polio vaccine.

Jonas had a creative way of thinking that made him different from other scientists. He sometimes imagined that he was a virus. He tried to think of how he would escape or trick a body's immune system. It really helped him understand how a virus worked.

To make a vaccine that could help a body fight off the poliovirus, Jonas and his team had to work in a creative way.

They had to find a way to kill the virus, but still leave something that the body would think was the virus, so it would try to fight the disease.

When he thought he had it right, Jonas tested the killed virus. He injected it into monkeys. Each monkey's body developed antibodies – special substances that help destroy disease – which meant it now knew how to fight off the virus.

It was exactly what Jonas had hoped would happen. He and his team had done what no other scientists could do.

Jonas often worked in his lab eighteen hours a day.

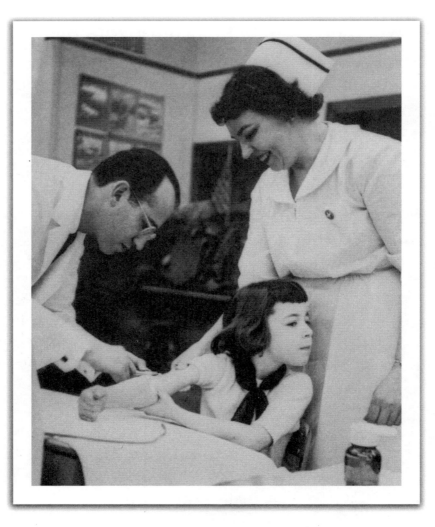

Jonas was always kind to children.
He never let them forget how important
they were to his work.

The next step was to see how the vaccine might work with children. The main problem was that Jonas didn't want any children to be hurt by his testing.

In May 1952, he began testing his vaccine on children who were already recovering from polio at the D. T. Watson Home for Crippled Children. Because they were recovering, these children already had antibodies to the disease. They couldn't get polio again, so the testing was safe.

Jonas made sure that he only gave children vaccines of the exact same kind of poliovirus they had already had. He took blood samples from the children before he gave the vaccine. Then he took new blood samples a few months later.

He was absolutely thrilled to find that the children had much higher levels of antibodies in their blood after receiving the vaccine.

Next, Jonas vaccinated volunteers from the children's families and workers at the Watson Home with a vaccine against all three types of polio.

None of these people had ever had polio. Their bodies had no antibodies. After they were vaccinated, not one of them became ill with polio – it was proof that Jonas's vaccine was safe!

The news got better and better. Jonas was careful to take blood samples from these volunteers months later. He wanted to see if the antibodies against polio were still in the people's bodies. The levels were just as high as they'd been during the earlier tests.

He had done it! His vaccine was safe, it worked, and it helped people stay immune to polio for at least one polio season.

*Collecting blood samples with
the help of a nurse's aide*

Testing across the U.S.

Jonas was delighted about his success with the vaccine. He shared his findings with other polio researchers at a meeting in January 1953. The NFIP decided to hold a nationwide test of the vaccine.

The day after the meeting, the new polio vaccine made headlines all over the world. People were desperate to stop polio.

Jonas was worried, though. He had wanted to keep quiet about the vaccine. He didn't want parents to get too excited too soon. The vaccine was not ready for public use.

Even worse, the hordes of reporters were getting in the way of his work. They disrupted his lab, taking pictures and talking to his staff.

Dr. Jonas Salk, in his lab

An enormous supply of vaccine was
needed for such a large experiment.

Jonas's laboratory couldn't make all the vaccine that was needed for the upcoming nationwide test. Jonas wrote up careful instructions for the drug companies that were going to produce the vaccine. He wanted to make sure the vaccine they made was both safe and strong enough.

On April 26, 1954, the biggest experiment in medical history began. Nearly two million children became **Polio Pioneers**. Almost half a million second-graders received the real vaccine, and 210,000 more received a **placebo** shot. More than a million first- and third-graders weren't given any sort of a shot at all – the scientists just watched them carefully during the time of the test.

To carry out this test, 20,000 doctors, 40,000 nurses, 50,000 teachers, and 200,000 other volunteers worked together.

It Works!

Jonas's friend Dr. Francis was asked to study the results of the test. Doctors and scientists back then didn't have computers. Because of this, it took Dr. Francis and his staff nearly a year to compare all of the different children's results.

Jonas Salk on a popular television news show, with its host, Edward R. Murrow

Dr. Thomas Francis, Dr. Jonas Salk, and Basil O'Connor (head of the NFIP) at a press conference

Finally, on the morning of April 12, 1955, Dr. Francis announced to the world that the Salk vaccine was not only safe, it also worked very well!

Millions of excited people heard the news on radio and television. Later that day, the government approved the vaccine so people could use it immediately. All children could now have polio shots and be free from fear.

Even though he didn't want a lot of attention, suddenly, Dr. Jonas Salk was a famous man.

He was flooded with letters and phone calls from all over the country. Over the years, he received many awards for his work. He was even invited to the White House, where he received a special award from the president.

He accepted the award "on behalf of *all* the people" who had worked to make the vaccine a success.

Dr. Jonas Salk and President Dwight D. Eisenhower

As soon as Jonas had won the battle against polio, he turned his attention to fighting other diseases.

He moved his family to La Jolla, California, in 1963. There, he started the Salk Institute for Biological Studies, a place where doctors and scientists could study problems and work together.

He believed that creative thinking led to scientific discoveries. He hoped his Institute might someday find a cure for diseases such as cancer or **AIDS**.

Dr. Salk and his second wife, artist Francoise Gilot, at the Salk Institute

Story Background

Dr. Jonas Salk made the world a safer place because of his work to stop the poliovirus.

Today, scientists at the Salk Institute are hard at work, trying to find a cure for AIDS. When he was in his seventies, Jonas began working on a vaccine to boost the immune system of people with the AIDS virus, so they wouldn't get full-blown AIDS.

Jonas Salk didn't live to see a victory over AIDS, but his work gave new hope to many patients. Today, people with the AIDS virus are living much longer, sometimes without ever showing signs of AIDS.

Jonas Salk could have been a wealthy doctor, but he chose instead to do the work that "made his heart sing." He continued to work part-time until his death in 1995.

*"Hope lies in dreams, in imagination
and in the courage of those who dare
to make dreams into reality."*

— Jonas Salk

Dr. Jonas Salk always believed that
if he asked the right questions, he could
find the answers.

Index

Glossary

AIDS – a virus that attacks a person's immune system, so he or she can't fight off disease and infection

bacteria – tiny, one-celled creatures that live in soil, water, plants, or animals

immune system – the body's way of fighting disease and infection

immunization – a shot that is given to a person to keep him or her from getting sick from a certain kind of disease

placebo – something a patient is told is a real medicine, but actually isn't. Often used for scientific testing and research.

Polio Pioneers – Dr. Salk's name for the children who were part of the first polio vaccine test

residency – a time when a doctor who has recently graduated begins to work, often for little or no pay

vaccine – something that teaches a body how to fight off a disease

virus – something that causes disease in plants or animals